THE HARP·KEY·

*Music for the
Scottish Harp
Arranged by*

Alison Kinnaird

KINMOR MUSIC
SHILLINGHILL, TEMPLE, MIDLOTHIAN, SCOTLAND

ISBN 0 9511204 0 9

Published by
Kinmor Music
Shillinghill, Temple, Midlothian, Scotland

Subsidised by the Scottish **A**rts Council

Printed in Scotland by
Bridgend Printers (Edinburgh) Limited
40 Constitution Street, Edinburgh EH6 6RS

ACKNOWLEDGEMENTS

My thanks are due to the many people who have helped in the work leading up to the production of this book.

- For their support and encouragement to my parents and to the late Jean Campbell; to William Matheson, Ann and Charlie Heymann, Col. Eoghan O'Neill and to Keith Sanger, all of whom were so generous with their information.

- For their help, in editing, correcting and transcribing the music, to David Johnson, Morag MacLeod and Nancy Bick Clark, and to Jill Morley for her beautiful hand-copying of the music.

- For typing all the notes and information, to Joyce McMillan.

- To all the harp players I know, and each of my pupils. I have learned something from them all.

- And especially to Robin.

INTRODUCTION

The small harp or clarsach is well known as one of the ancient traditional instruments of Scotland, but of the hundreds of tunes that must have been composed for it, most have been lost. The harpers do not appear ever to have written their music down themselves, so what has been handed down to us are tunes memorised by other musicians and put down on paper at a later date. What remains is usually a simple melody line. I have arranged some of these so that they are again playable on the clarsach and in a style suitable for the traditional background from which they come. They are not arranged for a particular standard of playing – each tune is given the treatment that it seemed to require. Some settings, therefore, are quite simple and some demand a good deal of technical skill. As well as those who play the clarsach, I hope that any reader will find the background to the tunes as fascinating as I do myself. Almost every piece of traditional music has a story linked with it. Knowing these historical links and the tales of tragedy, romance and intrigue that they involve make the music itself come alive. This, for me, is the fascination of traditional music – the tunes were composed by real people about real events which affected them greatly. The sorrow and joy, the anger, jealousy and pride come through in a way which is difficult to achieve with art-music.

More than 20 years ago when I began to learn the clarsach I was told that it was no longer possible to play traditional harp music. The harping tradition had been broken, in both Scotland and Ireland, at the end of the 18th century and, in Scotland, interest in the instrument did not revive until the end of the following century when Victorian romantics "discovered" Celtic music. The style of playing which was established then, much influenced by the "drawing-room" treatment of Scottish music by pianists such as Marjory Kennedy-Fraser, was still being taught when I first heard the instrument and is still taught today. It is, of course, a valid use of the clarsach and, in some ways, a very attractive style of playing, but its roots come from the classical tradition and not from the native tradition of Scottish music.

What makes a tune traditional? In some ways it is easier to start by ruling out some of the commonly accepted definitions. It is not simply age, because there is a great deal of good traditional music being composed today. Nor is it that the composer is unknown because we know many of the composers of traditional music, from hundreds of years ago to the present day. It is not just the fact that it has been handed down through a continuous oral tradition because a song which was written down a hundred years ago, and has not been heard since, can be sung today by a traditional singer and sound just as appropriate as those from an oral source. On the other hand, a traditional song when taken by a classically-trained singer will be changed into something quite different, even when they are singing the melody exactly as they hear it. The subtlety of timing and decoration will be lost and, importantly, the quality of the tone will be different. It may sound pleasing but it will no longer be a traditional piece of music. As the classical harpist Joseph Elouis (who was originally Swiss but lived for many years in Edinburgh) put it when discussing the fashionable 19th century arrangements of Scottish music – "That neither talents nor ingenuity can render such Accompaniments compatible with the Scottish Airs is strongly exemplified by those of the great Composer Haydn, which although replete with merit, give no idea of Scottish music; and for that reason, may be compared to a portrait exquisitely painted, but deficient in resemblance." Therefore, I think that the most important element in defining music as traditional is the style of performance, and this must come from continuous oral sources. It follows, then, that there is no reason why one cannot play traditional music on the clarsach – if one is aware of the native idiom of the music as played on other instruments. There has always been a constant exchange of ideas and techniques within the world of Scottish folk music in any case. The widespread adoption of pipe marches by the fiddle comes immediately to mind and, conversely, the performance of strathspeys on the bagpipes. Many musicians, in the past as well as today, have played more than one instrument or have been equally respected as singers, so it is inevitable that the style of playing on one instrument should influence the others. I am convinced, however, that the clarsach, when played traditionally, will sound as different in character from the concert harp as the fiddle does from the violin.

Becoming aware of the fine music being performed by traditional Scottish musicians – the various styles of Gaelic and Lowland singers, the bagpipes and fiddle music – I grew more and more dissatisfied with the music I had been offered to play on the harp. There is no way of knowing exactly how the harp was played 200 years ago since none of the harpers, either in Scotland or Ireland, ever wrote any of their music down themselves. On the other hand, many of their tunes were collected by pipers, fiddlers, flute-players and other musicians and are now played on other instruments. We also know that the pipes are not played in exactly the way that they were in the 18th century, nor is the fiddle. One would not expect the clarsach alone to remain static. The essence of traditional music is that it is a continuously evolving art form with each performer stamping their own personality on what they have inherited and taking it a little further. Attempting to recreate the music as it would have been heard 200 years ago would be a pointless (and hopeless) exercise in antiquarianism, and rather irrelevent in the context of a living tradition of Scottish music. In arranging the old tunes I have tried to do so in a style which seems to me to fit in with traditional music as it is played today.

Most of the tunes come from Scottish sources, though some are found in Ireland, and one came from a Canadian fiddle-player. The Gaelic bardic tradition of music and poetry was virtually a common one between Scotland and Ireland until the 17th century. It was in that century that the cultures of the two countries began to diverge. In Scotland this resulted in a Gaelic language with its own characteristics, which was spoken throughout the whole strata of Highland society. Along with this came a great flowering of poetry, song and instrumental music. A large amount of this is still current in oral tradition – many waulking songs, for example, date from this period. The harp, which was always very much a professional's instrument, and an instrument of the aristocracy, retained the Irish connection, and it was common for the harpers to travel to and fro between the two countries for instruction and performance. It is not surprising, therefore, that the same tunes turn up, sometimes under different titles, on both sides of the Irish Sea, and many Scottish harp tunes show the Irish forms of music, and probably vice versa.

The harp's link with the old Irish bardic tradition may have been one reason why it went out of fashion and its popularity waned at the end of the 17th century. Interest was growing in the new, peculiarly Scottish, forms of music and poetry. As with the rest of Highland culture, the point of crisis came with the 1745 Jacobite Rising when the chieftains who had supported the Stuart cause lost much of their power and wealth, if not their lives. Usually Catholic by religion, these chiefs often demonstrated a deep interest in their Gaelic culture and were patrons of their native arts. There is no doubt that political pressure and the lack of potential patrons also contributed to the disappearance of the harp from the Highlands. The same had happened 150 years earlier in the Lowlands, when the court of the Scottish kings moved to London, and the culture of the Lowland aristocracy became Anglicised. The harpers no longer played at the royal court or in the great houses of the nobles. Virtually no Lowland harp music has survived. I know of only one possible harp tune – "The Keiking Glasse" – which seems to have a specifically Lowland Scots title. The other handful of harp tunes which appear in Lowland sources seem to be attributed to Irish players. So it seems difficult to be at all certain about the repertoire of the Lowland harpers. Presumably they shared at least some music with their Irish and Highland contemporaries. Perhaps they would also have played music they heard played by other musicians of the day.

However, in the absence of any positive evidence connecting a tune to the clarsach, it would be pure speculation to claim that tune as part of its repertoire. That is not to say that the composition should not be played on the instrument. On the other hand, it seems important to me to establish a body of music which was actually composed for the clarsach. If nothing else, this may allow us to draw some conclusions about how the harp fitted into the old tradition. Almost all the pieces of music otherwise available when I began to learn the clarsach were arrangements of song tunes which did not really express the character of the harp as a solo instrument. Therefore I turned my search to the old collections of Scottish music, most of them from the 18th century, and thus written down within the lifetime, or at least within living memory, of the last harpers. One piece of evidence leads to another and I was amazed at how much music had, in fact, survived. As well as this, when other people became aware that I was looking for harp tunes they often kindly sent me anything they thought might be of interest, much of it very valuable to my research. Although much background and historical information has been given in the notes about each tune, new evidence is always coming to light which will help us understand more about the clarsach and its music.

All the tunes herein, except "The Lament for the Harp Key" and "Sheuglie's Contest" can be heard, as I play them, on my three albums :

"The Harp Key"   Temple Records SH001
"The Harper's Gallery" Temple Records TP003
"The Harper's Land"   Temple Records TP012
(duet album with Ann Heymann)

ARRANGING THE HARP TUNES

The main problem with putting the music into playable form is that it was usually written down as a simple melody line, occasionally with a single bass line below. In arranging the pieces for the clarsach, which is an instrument with obvious harmonic possibilities, it was important, in the first place, to consciously disregard the rules of classical harmony and the assumptions that these force one to make about the treatment of the music. Since I never studied as a pianist or concert harpist, perhaps I found it easier than it might have been if I were classically trained on these instruments. There are no rules laid down for dealing with traditional music, and harmony is very little used in the Scottish tradition except for the drones of the pipes and double-stopping on the fiddle. I found it useful to think of the clarsach in the first place as a melody instrument, and to create the harmonies to a large extent by decoration of the melody. The melody and the decoration are by far the most important elements in traditional music - harmony comes a very poor third but has to be used very carefully because it can so easily change the character of the music. It is very tempting to use the lush chords of the concert harp but I do not think these add anything to traditional tunes. A concert harpist to whom a friend of mine played some of my recordings said "But I could never play anything so simple"! I think this illustrates clearly the different approach one needs to take to the music. It does the melody no service to add a single note which does not allow it to be expressed better. The melody is all-important. Playing a melody well is hard! Indeed, I have found that my arrangements, over the years, have become more stark and honed-down leaving out all harmony notes which are not absolutely necessary. Clarity of the melodic line, rather than technical simplicity, is the end result.

Joseph Elouis again put it succinctly in the introduction to his first volume of music ... "It is generally allowed that modern embellishments or introductory and concluding symphonies added to Scottish Airs create want of unity which destroys their characteristic originality, and lovers of Scottish music observe with regret that most of the best melodies literally sink under the burden of foreign graces and intricate accompaniments. ... The following Accompaniments will betray no desire of shining at the expense of the subject, they contain no arpeggios nor showy passages (for the author considers such as incompatable with the simplicity of Scottish song)." Once again I would prefer to use the word "clarity" rather than "simplicity" as anyone will know who has attempted to transcribe the subtleties of a Gaelic song as rendered by a traditional singer.!

In discussion with other harpers such as Ann Heymann and Maire Ni Chathasaigh, whose music I enjoy, I find that we have come to many similar conclusions about the treatment of the music. I use octaves a great deal which adds depth and richness to the melody. In a chord I would usually play the octave notes, often with the lowest note used as a grace-note, and the fifth. I rarely include the third in the bass of an important chord. In this way "space" is left for the melody - a space which is all too easily cluttered with unnecessary notes. It is important to remember that the harp is constantly ringing, even if you damp the notes played, because the whole instrument resounds in sympathy with itself. This is obvious on the wire-strung harp but we often forget that the gut-strung harp is behaving the same way. I find that with a good arrangement, which allows the harp space to ring, the whole instrument begins to "sing" in the way that a well-tuned set of pipes does. I think it must be to do with the harmonics which the ringing strings set up. Often I only use single bass notes as harmony, and also find it useful, especially in dance music, to treat the harmony as a counter-melody, including decoration. This can be particularly effective as a bass line. Edward Bunting stated that harpers at the Belfast Harp Festival in 1792, who played in the old style, broke their chords downwards, beginning from the melody note. This is useful as it is not often used in classical music and gives a different "feel" to the harmony as a result, especially as it emphasises the melody much more that a chord spread upwards. These broken chords can be seen in the arrangements of "Caoineadh Rioghail" or "Bas Alastruim".

The use of decoration is essential in giving a tune its traditional character. There are no rules for adding decoration and its use varies from place to place. The Lewis style of Gaelic singing, for instance, is very much more decorated than that of Barra at the other end of the chain of islands in the Outer Hebrides. Now that modern recording techniques are making music from all areas more accessible and widespread, the regional differences are disappearing to a certain extent and decoration is more a matter of individual taste. There are infinite ways of decorating a tune but I will list a few of the graces that I find most useful, and some of the tunes where they are obviously used. Listening to the treatment given to decoration by singers, pipers, flute and fiddle players is essential to hear the whole range of possibilities for decoration, many of which also fit well on the harp. It is also the only way to acquire "an ear" for when and where to use decoration in a melody.

When they are familiar with the traditional idiom, players should be able to add their own decoration to tunes. I have noted down where it is essential to use the decoration exactly as written. The decoration should never be entirely removed from a melody.

CARRILL'S LAMENT

Single grace-notes, almost always played before the beat, as are most graces.

THE BATTLE OF SHERIFF MOOR

Single octave grace-notes give a lovely ring to the melody.

RORY DALL'S PORT

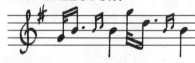

Double grace-note. Can be used to create a melody . . .

CARRILL'S LAMENT

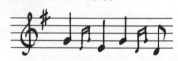

. . . as here, especially if the 3rd or, more rarely 4th is used.

RORY DALL MORISON

Consecutive triplets are an obvious grace to use on the harp, and are equally successful running up or down.

LAMENT FOR THE BISHOP OF ARGYLE

Non-consecutive triplets can also create a chord.

MacDONNELL'S MARCH

A Shake or Birl is more effective fingered 123 or 121 (or 131 or 141) on the gut harp than 222 with the front, back, front of the finger or nail which is so successful on the wire-strung harp. It can also be played 432 or 321.

HI RI RI RI HO

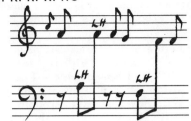

The effect of rapid repeated notes can be given very well by using both hands and taking one note in the lower octave. The ear assumes that the notes are all the same.

PORT ATHOLL

A turn – two grace notes linking descending notes. A very common decoration.

LAMENT FOR THE BISHOP OF ARGYLE

Bagpipe-style triplets create a harmony and only need the melody reinforced in the lower octave. Sometimes called a "throw" or a "grip".

LAMENT FOR THE BISHOP OF ARGYLE

The same type of decoration using only octave notes.

LAMENT FOR THE HARP KEY

With a wide spread of grace notes, easily achieved on the harp, no harmony is needed. This bar is built almost entirely on the same note in different octaves.

ELLEN'S DREAMS

A run of notes. I never use a glissando, which I think sounds very classical. It rings messily afterwards. I prefer to finger each note separately which gives more control.

On the whole, grace-notes should be played so quickly that the individual notes are barely perceptible. Again, listening to pipers, fiddlers or singers will give a guide to how they should be played. Grace-notes should never interrupt the flow of melody.

A general comment about tone. The soft and soothing nature of harp music is obvious and seductive. It is important to cut through the echoes of "Celtic Twilight" to the mainstream of the tradition and rid the harp of a stereotyped image which, I fear, contains some of the worst elements of backward-looking Scottish romanticism, a dead-end as far as energy and creativity are concerned. However, the strength of the harp has too often been ignored. It can be played with drive and bite - in other words with "guts", if you will excuse the pun. Neither aspect should be ignored.

With traditional music, I have found that the elbows are not raised as high as taught for the concert harp, that the hands are turned in slightly more, and that the strings are plucked nearer the tips of the fingers than with concert harp technique. This gives a brighter, slightly metallic edge to the notes. Setting the fingers on the notes before they are played is not such an important feature and is sometimes impossible if decoration is to be achieved. Having said that, the strength of the melody and the emphasis on the rhythm are vital, and as much bite and attack as is suitable for the melody should be given. These technical points have been gradually discovered from practical experience and I notice them used by other musicians who play the music in a traditional style. There is no right and wrong way to play the clarsach. Good technique is the vehicle which enables one to express the music in the best possible way, and does not restrict the performance because of the physical limitations of the musician. We are very much on a voyage of discovery as far as treatment of traditional music on the clarsach is concerned and the only guide-line I follow is that if it sounds good and feels comfortable, do it that way! Though these tunes were arranged for the gut-strung harp, we have found many of them can transfer, with little alteration except re-fingering for dampening the notes, to the wire-strung harp.

These are only a few of the harp tunes that I have come across in my researches. I have listed the most important sources and I hope that other players will be encouraged to make their own arrangements of these and the many other tunes which survive. It is very exciting to be involved with this wonderful instrument at a time when it is showing remarkable vitality, and interesting so many people. It is an ancient instrument with a history of royal dignity, romance and magical power which stretches back for a thousand years of Scottish history. Judging by the enthusiasm shown for it today, its future is also assured.

THE MUSIC

1. McLoud's Salute

2. **Ge do theid mi do m'Leabaidh** (Though I go to my bed)

 = 84

3. **Cumh Easbig Earraghaal** (Lament for the Bishop of Argyle)

15

4. **Bas Alastruim** (The Death of Alasdair)

5. MacDonnell's March

♩. = 78

Final chord

21

6. Killiekrankie

♩ = 138

7. **Caoineadh Rioghail** (Royal Lament)

♩ = 78

FINE   Variation

25

D.C. al Fine

8. Carrill's Lament

♩. = 78

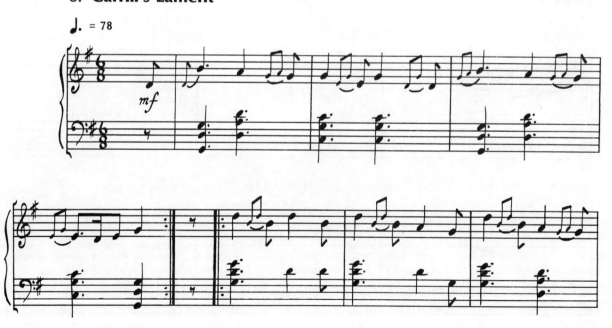

mf

9. Port Patrick

♩ = 80

Lively

10. **Hi ri ri ri ho** (The Harper's Land)

Variation 1

Variation 2

11. The Battle of Sheriff Moor

12. Blar Sliabh an t-Siorradh

♩. = 92

12a. Blar Sliabh an t-Siorradh (optional part for 2nd clarsach)

13. Rory Dall's Port

37

38

14. Port Atholl

♩ = 69

Slow

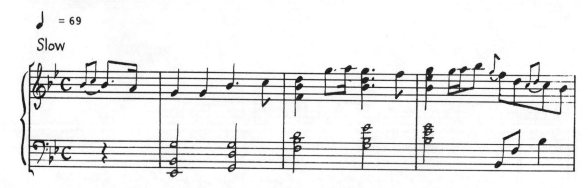

15. **Ruairidh Dall**—Jig

16. Suipeir Tighearna Leoid—(Lude's Supper)

♩ = 88

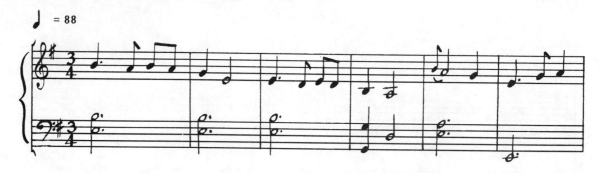

FINE

Variation
QuicK

17. **Fuath nam Fidhleirean** (Contempt for Fiddle Players)

18. **Cumha Peathar Ruaidhri** (Lament for Rory's Sister)

48

19. Far-fuadach a' Chlarsair (The Harper's Dismissal)

20. **The Lament for the Harp Key** (Cumha Crann nan Teud)

Variation 1

Variation 2

Variation 3

D.C. al Fine

21. Ellen's Dreams

22. The Braidwood Waits

58

23. Sheuglie's Contest betwixt his Harp, Fiddle and Pipes

Fiddle

Lowland Pipes
(E♭ drone)

Clarsach

D.S. al Fine   FINE

61

24. The Keiking Glasse

♩ = 128

Fiddle

Viola

Clarsach

Harpsichord

Clarsach

Harpsichord

Fiddle

Clarsach

Harpsichord

Fiddle

Viola

Clarsach

Harpsichord

1. McLoud's Salute

John Bowie published "A Collection of Strathspey Reels" in 1789. This is of interest particularly because of the small collection of harp tunes at the end, which he took down from the fiddle playing of a member of the Robertson family of Lude, in Perthshire. The Robertsons of Lude were well-known as patrons of the harpers. Their home had become, it seems, something of a magnet for visiting harpers because they had in their possession the two ancient clarsachs known as the Queen Mary Harp and the Lamont Harp. It is through the custodianship of the Robertson family and their successors that these instruments have survived and can now be seen in the National Museums of Scotland in Queen Street in Edinburgh.

Many legends have grown around the two harps. The Queen Mary Harp is said to have been presented to Beatrix Gardyn, of Lude, by Mary, Queen of Scots, when on a hunting party in Athol. This harp is of a similar type to the one known as "Brian Boru's Harp" in Trinity College, Dublin. Tradition has it that the Irish harp belonged to the King of Ireland who was killed at the Battle of Clontarf in 1014, but this seems unlikely. In fact, the Queen Mary Harp, like the Brian Boru harp, seems to date from the 15th century. Because of the frequent repetition of the symbol of the cross, and the letters D.O. (Deo Oblata) in the carving, this instrument may have been associated with the nearby church of Dunkeld, one of the most important centres of Christianity in Scotland, and have become linked in name with Mary, Queen of Scots, because her portrait, in enamels, was at one point attached to the pillar. Portraits of the reigning monarch were quite commonly fixed to instruments given as ceremonial objects or used in a courtly context. Bunting suggests that the Queen Mary Harp is the one mentioned by Arthur O'Neill in his account of Ruairi Dall O Cathain's death. O'Neill says that O'Cathain died in Scotland at a nobleman's house, leaving his harp and tuning key. The nobleman, named in other sources as MacDonald of Sleat, subsequently gave the key to Echlin O'Kane. Bunting suggests, with no apparent evidence, that O'Kane's harp came into the possession of the Robertsons but this seems to be purely an invention of his own. In the nineteenth century the harps passed by marriage into the ownership of the Stuarts of Dalguise. Incidentally, this may have been when it was seen by the writer, Beatrix Potter, who told in her diary of a childhood holiday when she was taken to a house called Stewartfield, where she relates that the caretaker opened a cupboard to show them a little harp which he said belonged to Queen Mary.

The Lamont Harp is said to have come from Argyle with a daughter of the Lamont family who married a Charles Robertson of Lude about 1460. However there is no Charles Robertson in the main line of Lude up till 1518, when the superiority passed out of Robertson hands. The title passed, about 120 years later, to an Alexander Robertson who appears to be descended from John Tarlachsone (Charles's son) and it seems likely that it was John's grandfather who married Lamont's daughter. A document of 1588 names a witness, Anthony McEwin VcChlairser, who is described as a servant of John Tarlachsone alias Robertson. Ronald Black suggests that Anthony is probably a scribal attempt at "Athairne", a name used by the McEwen family in Argyle, and also by the Irish family of O'Hosey bards. The McEwens seem to have remained as hereditary harpers to the Robertsons, at least until 1670 when the Lude Barony Court records that John McEwin harper brought a claim of assault agains Allan McDod who confessed "that he strak him with ane tree". Another fascinating fact is that the mother of Niel Gow, the famous fiddle player, was apparently a McEwen. Niel was employed as a musician in the Atholl household in the same area of Perthshire as Lude. Some of his fiddle compositions are reminiscent of known harp melodies. (For instance it is interesting to compare "Port Lennox" with Gow's "Lament for James Moray of Abercairney".) Perhaps his mother was of the same McEwens mentioned above, and might have been a source of some of his musical inspiration.

Several of the Robertson family are known to have played the harp themselves and this tune was apparently one of these handed down by them. The composition of a tune as a Salute or Welcome is also well known as a convention on the pipes.

2. Ge do theid mi do m'Leabaidh, 's beag mo shunnd ris a' chadal
(Though I go to my bed, I get little sleep)

One of the duties of the clan harpers was apparently to play the clan to sleep at night. The pipers, it seems, roused them in the mornings. The soothing quality of the clarsach was well-established. Several Irish writers mention the "Suantraighe" (sleep-inducing music) which was one of the three "feats" of Irish harping. The others were "Geantraighe" (gay or romantic music) and Goltraighe (melancholy music). The harpers seem to have used their talents to good effect, though not always with the best of motives. A story which dates back probably to the mid 17th century tells of an Irish harper Cailean Cormac, or Mac O'Chormaig, who fell in love with the daughter of his host, MacLeod of Lewis, when he was visiting his home during a tour of Scotland. Intending to murder MacLeod and abduct the girl, he lulled the household to sleep with an entrancing tune, which John Mackenzie, in "Sar-Obair nam Bard", tells us was called "Deuchainn-ghleusda Mhic O Charmaig" or MacCormac's Tuning-Tune. Just as he was about to cut his host's throat, however, MacLeod's son arrived in time to stop him.

The Lochmaben harper, in the Border ballad of the same name, employed his talents to help with the theft of a horse from the English Warden of Carlisle. He exhausted the entire company with dancing to his music. Then " . . . aye he harped, and aye he carped till a' the nobles were fast asleep", whereupon he crept down to the stables and stole the Warden's prized mount.

In a version of the Arthurian romance "Am Bron Binn", which Calum Johnston sang to me in Barra, the hero, Sior Bhoilidh, finds the beautiful woman, of whom the King of Britain had dreamed, a prisoner in the house of a giant. In order to escape she lulls her captor to sleep with the music of her harp " . . . An cuir thu do cheann air mo ghluin, 'S gun seinninn duit ciuil a 's cruit". At which point she and Sior Bhoilidh cut off his head.

If this melody is a harp-tune, the harper obviously had rather less success! It comes from Patrick McDonald's "A Collection of Highland Vocal Airs" (1784). Patrick McDonald was carrying on the work of his brother, Joseph, who had died on a voyage to the East Indies. He collected music in Perthshire, the Western Isles and Argyllshire to add to Joseph's collection which had been gathered mostly in Ross and Sutherland. Patrick is probably the "Mr. Macdonald" who allowed the MacLean-Clephane sisters to copy his manuscript collection of harp music "taken down from the playing of O'Kain by Mr. Macdonald".

He certainly was very interested in harp music. In the preface to the 1784 edition he describes some of the airs in the collection "as probably being the most genuine remains of the ancient harp-music of the Highlands". He laments the passing of interest in the harp both in Ireland and in Scotland and, in particular, in the old style of harping. He has obviously heard enough of this style of playing in Ireland to be able to contrast it with the modern treatment of the same tunes, which he considers much inferior. Echlin O'Kane is known to have been taught by Lyons, who played in the old style. One of the tunes in the MacLean-Clephane manuscript, "The Lady in the Desart" is also mentioned in Macdonald's forword to his collection. "The Lady in the desart, as played by an old harper, and as played according to the sets now in fashion, can hardly be known to be the same tune . . . The variations are such, as might have been composed, at this day, in Italy or Germany". However, McDonald does say that the harp has been seldom heard in Scotland for upwards of a century. He also presumably subscribes to the opinions put forward in the essay on Highland music contained in his 1784 edition which was " . . . generously communicated to him, by an ingenious friend . . .". It makes the statement that the contrast between the pipe and harp tunes is so striking that one could hardly imagine them to be the music of the same people – which is so demonstrably untrue that it makes one wonder about the other views expressed in his writing. "Ged do theid mi do m' leabaidh" is the type of tune that he describes as "genuine remains" and, while it may indeed have been played on the harp, it probably had words to it as a song as well.

3. **Cumh Easbig Earraghaal** (Lament for the Bishop of Argyle)

Some time between 1721-1727 the poetess Sileas na Ceapaich wrote a poem to lament the death of a harper called Lachlann Dall Mackinnon. He was a frequent visitor to their family home in Keppoch. She describes how much she valued his company, both as a source of news, which the travelling harpers were well-placed to carry round the countryside, and for his music. She says –

> "Nuair a ghlacadh tu do cheile 'S a bhiodh tu 'ga gleusadh lamh rium, Cha mhath a thuigte le h-umaidh Do chur chiuil 's mo ghabhail dhan-sa; Bu bhinn do mheoir air a cliathaich 'Nuair a dh'iarrainn Cumha 'n Easbuig, Cumha Ni Mhic Raghnaill lamh ris, Cumha Mairi 's Cumha Ghilleasbuig."

When you took your loved one and were tuning it beside me, a fool would not have understood very well your making of music or my reciting of poems. Your fingers were sweet on its side when I would ask for Cumha 'n Easbuig, Cumha Ni Mhic Raghnaill as well, Cumha Mairi and Cumha Ghilleasbuig.

The first tune she names may be the melody which appears in Daniel Dow's Collection (c1775). Colm O'Baoill says that another tune called Easbuig Erra-ghaidheal - The Bishop of Argyle - appears in the Angus Fraser M.S., but it is in fact a variant of the same melody. Yet another tune titled Cumh Easpuic Erra-ghaoidheal in the Walter McFarlan M.S. (1742) has only a slight resemblance to the other two. I chose to arrange a theme and two variations from Dow's version.

There are two Bishops for whom this tune may have been written. One is John Campbell, who was a second son of the house of Cawdor. He was Bishop of the Isles but there is some doubt as to whether he ever held the title of Bishop of Argyle. His predecessor, John Carswell, had accepted that appointment from the Catholic Mary, Queen of Scots, which was not viewed with favour by the newly reformed church in Scotland. After Carswell's death the Bishopric was allowed to lapse for a number of years - how long is not certain. We do know that John Campbell had a personal harper named David Macfie to whom he made a bequest in his will when he died, c1590.

The other possible candidate was Hector Maclean (1605-87) who became Bishop of Argyle in 1680. He came from Mull, an island with a strong harping tradition. He became a well-known figure, to the extent that his son Anndra, a poet, was identified as Mac an Easbuig - the Bishop's son.

There were harpers attached to the households of several clerics. The Royal Accounts of 1506-1507 show payments to "the Beshop of Ros harpar, . . . the beshop of Caithnes harper . . ." and "to the ald Priour of Quhithirnis clarscha". (Whitehorn).

The decoration in this tune must be played as written as it forms an integral part of the harmony.

The illustration shows carved lintel on a 17th century fireplace in Cawdor Castle, one of the Campbell family homes.
By kind permission of the Earl of Cawdor.

4. Bas Alastruim (The Death of Alasdair)

This version of the tune "Bas Alastruim" (The Death of Alasdair) was given to me in Ireland by Col. Eoghan O Neill. It comes from an unpublished manuscript which was collected by a member of his family and is dated 1780. This appears to be the earliest recorded version. The tune was also published by Crofton Croker (Researches in the South of Ireland, 1824) and a version as played by the Kerry pipers, by Canon Goodman, in his own M.S. in 1862. The longest version, which includes descriptive sections on the battle, the slaughter and the subsequent lamenting, was included in an essay by Francis Keane, written for a competition organised in 1876 by the Royal Irish Academy.

Alasdair Mac Cholla Chiotaich MacDonnell was leader of the Highland and Irish troops during Montrose's Rising in support of Charles I. He was the son of Colla Ciotaich (left-handed Coll) a figure well known in Highland history and music. Alasdair fought both in Scotland and Ireland for the Royalist cause, and after the fall of Montrose returned to Ireland where he took a command under Lord Taafe at the Battle of Cnoc na nDos in Co. Cork in 1647. He was surrounded when reconnoitring and surrendered on the promise of quarter. An officer gave a contemporary account of his death - "At which time comes up one Major Pardon, after baronetted, and demanded the Cornet who it was he gave quarters to. On which he told him; on which Pardon was in a fury and shot MacDonnell in the head being the other's prisoner, and so MacDonnell was lost. In revenge of which the Cornet for seven years fought Pardon every year but most commonly got the worse which the more was the pity . . . The loss of this field was much attributed to the want of ready conduct, and those on the right hand did not fight so vigorously as MacDonnell did on the left hand; but it was his Destiny to be so lost after these many fights and dangers he was in, in the wars of Scotland, being as stout and strong a man as ever carried a broad sword and targett of late days, and so vigorous in fight that had his conduct been equivalent to his valour, he had been one of the best generals in Europe."

The news of Alasdair's death is said to have been brought to Scotland by a harper who landed from Ireland at Portpatrick and told the sad tidings to the Gaelic poet Iain Lom. Iain Lom himself had served as guide to Alasdair before his victory at Inverlochy in 1645 and as bard on that occasion. He pointed out to Alasdair that he would be better able to compose suitable verses to commemorate the battle if he were able to view the combat from a safe vantage point rather than be involved in the actual fighting!

5. MacDonnell's March

In 1615 Colla, Alasdair's father captured a ship belonging to Henry Robinson of Londonderry and pressed some of the sailors into service for the return journey to Islay. Among these sailors was Robert Williamson, who described how they then travelled to Canna and were entertained by Clanranald. He says "There they went ashore and feasted and drancke with there friends and chieflie with McCallan, O Cathan his wife, her husband then being in Scotland". Ronald Black suggests that the O Cathan mentioned is Ruairi Dall O'Cathan (the other chiefs of that name all being in prison at that time). Ruairi appears to have travelled to the mainland while his wife remained in Canna as the guest of Clanranald (Mac 'ic Ailean). Was Ruairi then perhaps the harper who brought the news of Alasdair's death back to Scotland?

Edward Bunting's collection "The Ancient Music of Ireland" contains this tune which is again linked with Alasdair Mac Cholla Chiotaich. It also appears in O'Neill's (1850) and in Pat Mitchell's "Dance Music of Willy Clancy" (1976). According to Gratton Flood, it was played on the warpipes by Alasdair's troops at their leader's funeral. It may originally have been a pipe-tune, but it has been taken up by the harp with great success. Ann Heymann and I recorded it as a duet. She has been playing it for a number of years, and I was so impressed with the tune that I made my own arrangement, giving it a somewhat different treatment for the gut-strung harp.

According to "The Clan Donald" (A. & A. MacDonald), Alasdair's great-great-grandson, James MacDonnell, had a deep interest in Irish traditional music and did much to encourage Edward Bunting in his collection of old harp music.

6. Killiekrankie

I learned this version of "Killikrankie" from a fiddle player called Gillies who told us that in the part of Nova Scotia where he lived the style of fiddle playing was said to have derived from that of the old harpers. It is possible that exiles who left Scotland at the time of the Jacobite Risings were familiar with the music of the harpers but, whether this is true or not, it is particularly interesting that the Nova Scotians placed a value on keeping this tradition alive.

Killiekrankie has a very mixed musical pedigree. It is related to many other tunes going back to the early 17th century. In England it relates to "The Clean Contrary Way", "Gilderoy" and the "Miller of Dee" which were played on bass viole, viole and virginal and also sung. As "Gilliecrankie" it appears in Oswald's "Caledonian Pocket Companion" and was also set for violin and continuo by William MacGibbon (1695-1756). In Ireland it is also related to the "Star of the County Down" and the Gaelic song "Gleanntan Araiglin Aobhinn", and is found in the Atkinson manuscript of 1694/1695 as "The Irish Gillycranky".

The brothers Thomas and Laurence O'Connellan were harpers who came to Scotland at the end of the 17th century and Thomas is credited with having composed this tune, sometimes referred to as "Planxty Davis". This title seems to have been attached to the tune by mistake, and probably instead belongs to a tune to which O'Carolan wrote words - "The Two William Davises". Thomas is said to have settled in Edinburgh sometime around the 1690's and may have been rewarded for his harp playing by being appointed a Burgess of the city. The Edinburgh Council Records of January, 11th, 1717, note that "the Council appointed the Dean of Guild and his Council to admitt and receave Thomas Occulay, harper" and two others to be "burgesses in Common forme". Colm O'Baoill suggests that Occulay is a misspelling of Oconlan and this would seem to confirm the version of O'Connellan's life in Arthur O'Neill's "Memoirs". It was not unknown for musicians to be honoured in this way - an oboist, Malcolm MacGibbon (possibly the father of William MacGibbon referred to above) was made a burgess because of his musical prowess in 1696. Some sources may that O'Connellan returned to Ireland and some that he died in Edinburgh.

The tune "The Braes of Killiekrankie", to which Robert Burns put words, is not related to the O'Connellan melody. Both are probably called after the Battle of Killiecrankie which was fought in Perthshire in 1689 between the Highland forces led by Claverhouse in support of the Catholic James II and the Protestant Major-General Mackay leading the army of William III.

7. **Caoineadh Rioghail** (Royal Lament)

The Royal Lament is one of the tunes associated with the Maclean family. This version is the theme and one variation from the Angus Fraser manuscript. It is also found in the Macfarlan manuscript and in Oswald's "Caledonian Pocket Companion". It is said to have been composed by John Garbh Maclean, Laird of Coll, on the execution of King Charles I in 1649. John Gunn, in "An Historical Enquiry respecting the Performance on the Harp in the Highlands of Scotland" (1807) says that two of his compositions "Caoineadh Rioghail" and "Toum Muran" (The Hill of Bent-grass) are known, however this latter seems now to have been lost. John Garbh died around 1685, at an advanced age, having apparently outlived his son and grandson, according to the manuscript genealogy compiled by Dr. Hector Maclean in the middle of the 18th century. The earliest mention of him was by an Englishman, the local governor, who wrote of John Garbh's prowess on the harp.

The Macleans of Coll were a family well known for their interest in the harp, right up to the 19th century. They were perhaps the last patrons to employ a harper in the household - a payment was made to Murchadh Clarsair (Macdonald) in 1734 and he subsequently retired to Quinish in Mull. His son and grandson worked on the Maclean estate after his death. The Maclean-Clephane sisters at Torloisk in Mull took a great deal of interest in harp music and compiled a manuscript which contains 36 Harp Airs which they probably obtained from the collection of Patrick Macdonald of Kilmore. It seems likely that the "O'Kane" from who he took down the tunes was Echlin O'Cathain b. 1729, an Irish harper who visited Scotland several times in the years up to 1790. Miss Maclean performed songs accompanying herself on the spinet for Dr. Johnson in 1773 and translated Gaelic poems for him. Later, c. 1815, Alexander Campbell visited her and obtained some harp tunes from her. She told him that she remembered Murchadh well and that these tunes were played by him.

8. **Carrill's Lament**

"Carrill's Lament" is found in James Oswald's "A Caledonian Pocket Companion" and has the same musical form - a series of short, related, phrases, almost variations - that many of the Irish/Scottish tunes of this period have in common. It may have been called after one of the Irish harpers whose names were known in Scotland, even if they had not visited the country themselves. Several tunes in Oswald's collection are called after O'Carolan, with a variety of spellings (e.g. Carland's Devotion, Currallan's Lament), and none of them appear to be compositions of his, or they certainly do not appear in any of the known collections of his work. It is more likely that they were simply named after him as a compliment, or, because they were nown to be harp tunes, they had the name of a famous harper attached to them.

Another alternative for the name would be the famous Irish family of musicians, the O'Carrolls or MacCerbhaill's. Maelrooney MacCerbhaill, chief musician of the kingdom, and his brother Gillakeigh - a famous tiompanist and harper - were killed in a massacre at Bragganstown, near Ardee, in 1329. Their descendants, Donlevy O'Carroll, who died in 1357, and Gillacuddy O'Carroll, who died in 1379, are also said to have been outstanding minstrels.

A tune which appears in an unpublished fiddle manuscript dated 1814 entitled "Paddy O'Carroll, with Variations" may also be a reference to the same musicians.

The melody of "Carrill's Lament" does not seem particularly sad. Bunting, in his notes on the characteristics of Irish melody which occur at the beginning of his "Ancient Music of Ireland" gives the definition of the word "Cumhadth - Lamentation" as "Time of the music composed in compliment to the deceased patrons of the harpers, without words, but by no means slowly played". It seems that a lament could sometimes be written to describe the character of the person who had died and thus was not necessarily dirge-like.

9. Port Patrick

Although most of the tunes named "Ports" are ascribed to Rory Dall, this one is not named by any of the collectors or oral sources as being one of his compositions. It occurs in Oswald's "A Caledonian Pocket Companion". It does not appear that it is connected with the little town of Portpatrick in Wigtownshire although, by coincidence, this was where the harper landed who brought the news of the death of Alasdair Mac Cholla Chiotaich to Scotland.

Patrick was, of course, a very common name and there are numerous instances of harpers called Patrick, Pate or Paddy. The Lord High Treasurer of Scotland records payments in the first decade of the 16th century to two harpers with this name. However, neither of them was the "Patrick Harper" murdered in Edinburgh in 1503 by a drummer called William Taburner who was declared a fugitive from the King's laws and put to the "horne". Patrick Quinn was one of the harpers who took part in the Belfast Harp Festival in 1792. As mentioned elsewhere, I also have a copy of a manuscript containing a melody, possibly a harp tune, entitled "Paddy O'Carroll". As now, it may have been quite common for Irishmen to be nicknamed "Paddy"!

In any case, this is a very pretty little tune, a slow air which does have a slight Irish feel about it, changing into a variation in jig time. I often return to the slow air at the end.

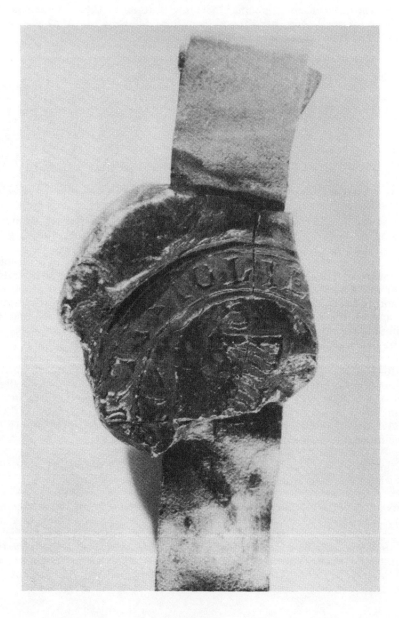

10. **Hi ri ri ri ho** (The Harper's Land)

The original title of this tune is that which is given in Oswald's "Caledonian Pocket Companion". It is simply a vocable description of the first bar of the melody, but I found it so awkward to say that I have given my arrangement the alternative title of "The Harper's Land".

The use of vocables to describe a tune which has so much in common with other harp tunes that I feel strongly that it may have been played on the harp is interesting. One might suggest that this gives a clue to how harp tunes might have been handed down. Certainly there must have been some way of transmitting them in a formalised manner because we know that the training of a harper was arduous, and took several years. Suggestions have been put forward about how it might have been written down, including the use of Ogam script, but the whole of Irish and Highland Scottish culture was very much based on oral tradition right up to the 18th century. There is no doubt that the bards and harpers had to develop their capacity for memorising information to an extraordinary degree, and it seems more likely that the tunes were passed on by some system like the canntaireachd of the bagpipes, where each note and musical motif has a syllable or sound to describe it, and a tune can thus almost be 'talked' through. We unfortunately have no clue as to how a harmony line would be dealt with, apart from the few named chords in the preface to Bunting's 1840 edition. Perhaps one day a "canntaireachd" manuscript for the harp will be discovered, as they have been for the pipes, and shed a new light on the subject!

I chose the title "The Harper's Land" because it was the name given to the part of a chief's or laird's estate where a harper would live, often rent-free, in return for his services. A "Harperland" near Dundonald in Ayrshire is on record as early as 1373, and was probably held by the harpers to the High Stewards of Scotland, Seneschals of the King's household. One of these harpers is mentioned in a message from King Edward II of England ordering that the Sheriffs of London should immediately release the "harpour" of the Steward of Scotland, whom they had arrested, despite the fact that he held a safe conduct which had been issued by Roger de Horsely, one of the English wardens of the uneasy truce on the March, or English/Scottish Border. The harpers, as in Ireland, were regularly used as messengers, envoys – and spies –in troubled times.

A harper's land, called Dalellachan, near Kirkmichael, was held by the personal harper of Robert the Bruce and was eventually sold by his descendants for twelve cows with calves. In the same area, near Kirkoswald, a Harperland, also known as Slaphouse, features in a document signed by Robert Jolly, its owner, in 1580. A broken fragment of the seal, still attached, bears a representation of a harp which closely remembles some Irish instruments. Elsewhere in the Lowlands are Harperrig near Calder, which was on record prior to 1586, and Harperfield in the parish of Lesmahagow, which existed before 1622.

In the Highlands there are numerous placenames connected with the harpers, such as Bail' a' Chlarsair (Harper's Town) at Waternish and Camas a' Chlarsair (Harper's Bay) at Applecross. Some castles are particularly associated with harpers like Kinkell Clarsach in the Black Isle where I was delighted to play at the celebrations marking its reconstruction. Totamor, in Glenelg, where the Blind Harper was given land was apprantly know as Tobhta a' Chlarsair in oral tradition, while Fanmor nan Clarsairean, in Mull, was held by the Harper to Maclean of Duart himself and not, as previously suggested, by the Harpers to the Macleans of Torloisk, who only bought the estate in the 19th century. Their harpers – the last to be attached to a Highland household – did live on their estate but the name exists in a document dating from the late 17th century, so it obviously refers to the earlier chieftainship.

The illustration shows a fragment of the Jolly seal, showing harp.
By kind permission of John Hamilton.

11. The Battle of Sheriff Moor

12. Blar Sliabh an t-Siorradh

12a. Blar Sliabh an t-Siorradh (optional part for 2nd clarsach)

Another tune from the group of harp music in John Bowie's collection, said to have come from the Robertsons of Lude.

Tradition has it that the harpers often followed their masters into battle, and there are some examples of which we know. Francis Collinson tells the story of the Earl of Argyll who took his harper with him to the Battle of Strathaven in 1594 to fulfill the prophecy of a witch who was apparently also a member of the Earl's household. She foretold that the harp would be played the day after the battle in Buchan. Argyll assumed that this signified that he would be victorious – he was wrong. It was played in Buchan, but as part of the captured spoils of his enemy, the Earl of Errol.

It seems unlikely that the harpers roused the armies to fight in the way that the Highland war-pipes were used, unless battles were on a very much smaller scale! In fact, the harpers, as bards, probably inspired the men with their words before a battle rather than their instrumental music. They also seem to have acted as messengers and spies to the extent that the nobility "within the English pale" in Ireland were banned from receiving them – legislation which was, happily, often ignored by the Anglo-Irish lords.

The oral historian Donald Macrury of Knockline, North Uist, tells us that at least one harper is said to have fought at Sheriffmuir in 1715. He was Donnachadh MacPhadruig (Duncan MacPhail) who died in North Uist in about 1795 at an advanced age, said to have been around 107 years. He may have been connected with the Macdonalds of Sleat as he is said to have composed a lament on the death of Ewen Macdonald of Vallay, a cousin of Sir Alexander Macdonald. Alexander's father, Sir Donald Macdonald, and his brothers fought a Sheriffmuir. Donald forfeited the chieftainship for his part in the Rising but it was restored to his heir in 1727.

Macdonald came down from Skye with 700 of his men to join the army of the Earl of Mar in support of James III, the Old Pretender, and they faced the Duke of Argyll at Sheriffmuir, near Dunblane. Though Mar's forces outnumbered Argyll's army by nearly three to one, and although the Highlanders on the right succeeded in routing Argyll's left wing, at the same time the left wing of their own army was put to flight. By the time darkness fell neither side had gained a decisive victory and this confusion is reflected in the Lowland Scots ballads of the day –

> "We baith did fight and baith were beat,
> And baith did rin awa, Willie" (Up & waur them a',Willie)

> "There's some say that we wan, and some say that they wan,
> And some say that nane wan at a', man". (The Battle of Sheriffmuir).

None of the songs, which name many of those who took part in the battle, mention a harper. A trumpeter called John Maclean was there and several pipers, and Donnachadh MacPhadruig may have been there in this latter capacity, since he is said to have played harp, pipes and fiddle. Other personalities mentioned elsewhere in this book who fought at Sheriffmuir were Alexander Robertson of Struan, poet and warrior, and Robert Stewart of Appin, who had married Iseabail MacLeod, daughter of Iain Breac.

The second tune, "Blar Sliabh an t-Siorradh" (The Battle of Sheriffmuir) caught my eye in the Angus Fraser manuscript because of the identical title. I have no reason to think it is a harp tune. It is probably a fiddle tune but it follows the other slow harp air very well, and it is perhaps appropriate to play two tunes of such different characters about the same subject, since it could be seen as both a victory and a defeat. Ann Heymann and I recorded it as a duet so I have adapted our arrangement for a simple second harp part, though the first harp can stand up just as well as a solo piece.

13. Rory Dall's Port

The confusion between Ruairi Dall O'Cahan and Rory Dall Morison existed for many years and several historians and musicians, including John Gunn and Edward Bunting, made the mistake of regarding the two harpers as the same person.

There is no doubt that they were two separate historical figures. Ruairi Dall O'Cahan was an Irishman who lived in the first half of the 17th century. Arthur O'Neill said that he was a chief of the O Cathain family, a nobleman who travelled through Scotland. Colm O'Baoill, in the Transactions of the Gaelic Society of Inverness, points out that none of the O'Cathain chiefs in the main line of the family would fit the description of the harper, either through their known history or the dates recorded of their deaths. He has found a different version of Ruairi's origins in "Dalriada : or North Antrim" by William Adams, published by "The Coleraine Chronicle" in 1906. This account, which probably comes from oral tradition, is as follows :

> "The last inhabitant of Dunseverick was Gilladuff O'Cahan, a very respectable gentleman, but unfortunately joined the insurrection of 1641, under Sir Phelim O'Neill of Tyrone, as was already stated. Gilladuff had two sons, Torlough, who was hanged with his father in Carrickfergus, and Rory Dall (or Blind Rory), who escaped to the Highlands, and is said to have changed his name to Morrison. He was a great musician - he could play on both harp and bagpipes. He was much respected by the Highland gentry, and was called 'Rory, the Irish harper'."

Ruairi is not mentioned elsewhere but we know that An Giolla Dubh and his son Toirrdhealbhach Og were executed at Carrickfergus in 1653 for their part as allies of Alasdair Mac Cholla Chiotaich in the insurrection of 1641. Another son, Manus, was also serving with Alasdair in Scotland and was hanged there after the Battle of Philiphaugh in 1644. There may also have been a further son, also called An Giolla Dubh. Whatever his ancestry was, Ruairi O'Cathan certainly spent a great deal of his life in Scotland and at least one of his tunes had been written down there by 1630. Most of the tunes described as 'Ports' have been ascribed to him.

There has been some discussion about the word 'Port' which nowadays simply means tune but at one point seems to have referred specifically to harp music. The tunes with 'port' in the title are of such different characters, though they usually have an assymetrical musical shape, that it does not seem to have been any particular type of tune. Like the Irish 'Planxty', which is associated with the harper-composers, it may just have been an instrumental piece of music quite separate from the dance tunes or songs which form the bulk of the Gaelic tradition.

Because Ruairi Dall is said to have composed several 'Ports' it is sometimes assumed that all the tunes with this title are his work. Most of the early ones possibly are, but the name does crop up from time to time in other tunes. "Port Patrick" in Oswald's "Caledonian Pocket Companion" is not credited to Rory Dall, nor is "Failte na Miosg", to which a manuscript in the National Library give the alternative title of "Port More". (This tune also occurs in several of the collections and manuscripts which are known to contain harp tunes). I also have a copy of a fiddle manuscript collected by Lt. Alexander Noble in 1814 which gives a tune called "Port Royal" which is a variant of "Jenny Dang the Weaver". (It is written down next to a tune called "Paddy O'Carroll" – could this be called after O'Carolan or Maelrooney MacCerbhaill? – and might have come from the same source.)

There are two tunes known with the title "Rory Dall's Port". The older one occurs in the Straloch manuscript and is reproduced in Johnson's "Scots Musical Museum". As the Straloch manuscript dates from 1627-29, this tune is clearly one of Ruairi Dall O'Cathain's. It is also found in the Skene manuscript under the title "Port Ballangowne". The other, which is the one I have arranged here, comes from Oswald's collection. Robert Burns wrote the original version of "Ae Fond Kiss" to part of this tune, and though it is not used for that song nowadays, an elderly lady once approached me after I had played it in a concert to tell me that she had learned Burn's song to this tune as a child at school. William Matheson points out that this is why "Hi ho ro 'sna ho ro eile", a Gaelic song to a variant of the melody now commonly used, has been attributed to Rory Dall.

James Oswald published several volumes of Scottish tunes between about 1745-1759 which are of great interest. He also composed many tunes himself, some original melodies and some variations on old themes. Many of these are ascribed to him in the collection but he also "improved" or expanded on some of the other tunes without ascription. It seems likely that this is one of these tunes. It is not known how much of it (if any!) is an original Rory Dall composition but several, at least, of the variations are probably Oswald's. David Johnson points out that by comparing some of the different occasions on which Oswald published it, it is possible to see where he cut out a couple of variations to fit it on to the printed page, and then stuck them in again at the end when he found there was room for them after all! However, he obviously supposed that he was composing a tune in the style of a harp tune.

In any case, it is one of my favourites and works extremely well as a piece of music, whatever its origins.

14. Port Atholl

This is one of the compositions attributed to Ruairi Dall O'Cahan. It is found in Oswald's "Caledonian Pocket Companion", from which this version is taken. A different tune, to which Carolan's poem "Seabhac Bheal Atha Seanaigh" could be sung, is also known as "Port Atholl", and is found in Bunting's 1840 edition and O'Sullivan's "Carolan" and there is also a version called "Port Atholl" in the 19th century Forde manuscript. Variants are also found in the collections of Daniel Dow and John Bowie.
It was common for musicians to dedicate a piece of music to the nobles for whom they played, especially the itinerant musicians who travelled round many of the "big houses", and this tradition has been carried on, particularly by the fiddle and bagpipes, up to the present day. There were several of the great families in Perthshire who took an interest in the harp and this tune may have been composed by Ruairi Dall for John Murray, firth Earl of Atholl, who died in 1642. Alternatively, the tune known in Ireland may be that composed by O'Cahan, while this one may have come from another source. John Murray himself employed a personal harper, a man named Alasdair Reid, who died in 1639. Perhaps this man, inspired by O'Cahan's example, made his own version of a "Port" for his master. Another harper called John Robertson was a pensioner of the Atholl estate in 1709, which is the last reference to a harper employed by the Atholl household.

15. **Ruairidh Dall**—Jig

This tune comes from the Angus Fraser manuscript. This was the second part of the collection that he made with his father, Captain Simon Fraser, but it was never published. Angus Fraser took a great interest in piobaireachd and harp music and had his own theories on its form and development. The manuscript contains a number of harp melodies but this tune, which is called after the most famous Highland harper, is probably a fiddle tune -somewhat ironic considering Rory Dall's opinion of fiddle players!

Ruairidh MacMhuirich, Rory Dall Morison, was the harper to the MacLeods of Dunvegan. He was born in Lewis around 1656 and was apparently blinded by small-pox as a child. Like many others, this led to his taking up music as a profession and he excelled at it. He is often referred to as "An Clarsair Dall" (The Blind Harper). He is said to have spent some time studying music in Ireland, which would accord with his father's estimation that it had cost him more to make a harper of Rory than to educate his two brothers to be ministers of the Church! He seems to have begun his career as an itinerant minstrel with a group of somewhat disreputable companions. In 1681, however, he met Iain Breac, chief of the MacLeods, who was in Edinburgh to pay court to James II. There then began a relationship of patron and dependant which lasted till Iain Breac's death in 1693 and resulted in the songs and music which have survived for us. Iain Breac was perhaps the last chieftain to keep a household which exemplified the final flowering of Highland culture. Dunvegan is described in the Blind Harper's songs as a house of unbounded hospitality which attracted poets and musicians as well as visitors of learning and culture, and it is not surprising that Rory Dall saw his stay in MacLeod's household as a golden period in his life. In 1688 he moved to Glenelg (of which more later) and from this time on his relationship with the MacLeods seems to have been more difficult, especially with the chief's successor, Rory Og MacLeod, whom he castigates in his "Lament for Iain Breac (Oran do MhacLeoid Dhun Bheagain)" for not upholding the traditional way of life and its virtues.

From 1693 onwards the Blind Harper is mostly associated with the MacLeods of Talisker, for whom he composed several songs and poems, and is mentioned by visitors to the household. After John MacLeod of Talisker's death in about 1700 he moved to live with his father-in-law in Lochaber. His wife, Catriona, seems to have been a determined woman who would lead her blind husband when travelling, as he apparently made occasional visits to several of the noble houses in the Highlands and Islands. In 1713 an entry in the accounts of John MacLeod of Contullich mentions purchasing a plaid for "blind Roderick", and tradition has it that the Blind Harper returned to Skye at the end of his life and was buried at Dunvegan. He was certainly dead before August 1714 when his brother, Rev. Angus Morison, uses the phrase "if poor Rorie were alive" in a letter to John Mackenzie of Delvine.

Rory Dall Morison was obviously a notable personality in his day, as is bourne out by the many sayings attributed to him and references made to him by other writers, musicians and bards. It is a great pity that so little of his instrumental music survives, though his songs, happily, were preserved in the oral tradition and are often sung today.

16. **Suipeir Tighearna Leoid**—(Lude's Supper)

The feasts held by the Highland chieftains were celebrations of unbounded hospitality with dancing, gaming and song and large quantities of roast venison and beef consumed, as well as wine and whisky. Bards, pipers and harpers were usually there, some travelling many miles to be in attendance, and often composed songs, poems or tunes especially for the occasion. Iain Lom describes one evening where two harpers were performing:

> "Is da chlarsaich an comhstri
> Gus am freagradh am balla
> Do mhac-talla nan organ
> Fion dearg Spaineach 'ga losgadh
> 'N cuid a dh 'obair nan orcheard"

> "Two harps vied with each other until the wall answered
> to the echo of organs, and red Spanish wine shone brightly
> in the handiwork of goldsmiths".

This comes from the "Lament for the Marquis of Huntly" who, as Colm O'Baoill suggests, is probably the Huntly to whom the harp tune "Port Gordon" was addressed.

The feasts were opportunities for the chiefs to demonstrate their magnificence and power. The story is told of MacLeod (perhaps Alasdair Crouchback) who was condescendingly asked, by a Lowland noble, if he were not impressed by everything he saw during a splendid dinner at the Scots Court. To this sneer MacLeod answered that he had a finer hall, table and candlesticks at home. Not surprisingly, this aroused the King's curiosity and during a Royal Visit to the Highlands (probably in 1540) he wished to see the wealth of which MacLeod had boasted. Unexpectedly, they were conducted to the top of two flat topped hills, known as MacLeod's Tables, where, amid spectacular views across sea and mountain, stood the finest stalwart clansmen holding aloft blazing torches. In these surroundings the feast was served. The chieftains often showed a certain sense of style!

"Suipeir Tighearna Leoid" is said to have been composed by Ruairi O'Cathan on a visit to the Robertsons of Lude around 1650. The Laird of Lude at this time was Alexander Robertson (c1618–73). If the date is correct (it was given to John Gunn), it would obviously rule out Rory Dall Morison as the composer. But Gunn's facts are not reliable and, as the Robertsons continued their interest in the harp right into the 18th century, the authorship of the tune is still in doubt. It is the only one of the "Ports" attributed to O'Cahan which goes into a variation but, since the variation occurs in Oswald's collection and he was inclined to invent his own variations, this cannot be taken as particularly meaningful evidence.

The last Irish harper to visit the Robertsons was Denis O'Hampsey, of Hempson. He probably played for both Robertson of Struan in about 1725 and John Robertson of Lude. Lude showed him a small harp which his father had played on, which O'Hampsey restrung for him. Though Robertson invited him back to teach his three year old son to play, O'Hampsey never returned to Lude.

James Macintosh tells of a visit he made to John Robertson's father, also called John. Lude showed him two harps, one of which he said had belonged to Queen Mary. "James", said Lude, "Here are two Harps: the largest one is the loudest, but the small one is the sweetest; which do you wish to hear played?". Macintosh chose the smaller one. Lude took up the harp and played till daylight. One of the tunes which he played was this one – "Suipeir Tighearna Leoid".

The illustration shows Bard and Harper performing for the chief of the MacSweynes. John Derick – Image of Ireland 1581.

A Now when into their fencedholdes, the knaues are entred in,
   To smite and knocke the cattell downe, the hangmen doe beginne.
   One plucketh off the Oxes cote, which he euen now did weare:
   Another lacking pannes, to boyle the flesh, his hide prepare.
C These theeues attend vpon the fire, for seruing vp the feast:
B And fryer smelfeast sneaking in, doth picace amongst the best,

3 who playeth in Romish toyes the Ape, by counterfetting Paull:
   for which they doe award him then, the highest roome of all.
   who being set, because the cheere, is deemed little worth:
   Except the same be intermixt, and lac'de with Irish myrth.
D Both Barle, and Harper, is prepared, which by their cunning art,
   Doe stirre and cheare up all the gestes, with comfort at the hart.

17. **Fuath nam Fidhleirean** (Contempt for Fiddle Players)

This is one of the tunes traditionally associated with Rory Dall Morison. It comes from Daniel Dow's Collection and, in that, it is ascribed to "Rorie Dall", while the other tunes in the collection which are associated with the Irish Ruairi Dall O'Cathain have no ascription. William Matheson argues a case that this tune could be the composition of An Clarsair Dall. This would certainly fit in with what we know of Rory Dall's opinion of fiddle playing. The MacLeod household in the late part of the 17th century was a notably musical one. Not only did it contain Morison and, presumably, his pupils, since we know that he taught the harp, but Patrick Mor MacCrimmon (c1640-70) and Patrick Og MacCrimmon, who were the hereditary pipers. Iain Dall Mackay, the Blind Piper, was also a friend of Rory's. Indeed, Iain Breac, according to Ramsay of Ochtertyre, was one of the last Highland chiefs to number among his retinue bard, harper, piper and fool.

In the MacLeod accounts of 1683-84 there is mention of a fiddle player employed in the chief's household for the first time. This was James Glass to whom the Harper refers as "an Gall Glas" (Glass the Lowlander). The fiddle was beginning to take over in popularity from the ancient harp and this was obviously resented by the harpers. Donald Macintosh, in his 1785 edition of "A Collection of Gaelic Proverbs and Familiar Phrases" quotes the proverb "Mas ceol fidileireachd tha na leor againn dhith" and tells us that "Roderick, a famous harper, met with a man who played every tune upon the violin, which Roderick played upon the harp, a thing not common in those days, which made the harper repeat the above words (now become a proverb) meaning that he did not reckon the violin music but, if it was, he had enough of it". William Matheson points out that "Roderick" is only named as "Rory Dall, alias Roderick Morison" in the second edition of Macintosh's book, which perhaps gives it less credence, but Matheson gives a traditional version of the proverb in his own book "Masa ceol fidileireachd, tha gu leor siod dheth". The Blind Harper is again supposed to have said this on hearing a fiddler performing music usually played on the harp. This tune certainly seems to me to express this dislike very strongly.

Sarcastic poems intended as insults were quite common in Gaelic literature and there are many examples of bardic contests in verse. Indeed their words could apparently be so vitriolic that they were said to have been able to raise a rash on the face of their opponent. Rory Dall himself was adept with words as well as music but does not seem to have got the better of Clanranald's bard, Donald MacVurich. William Matheson in his book "The Blind Harper" quotes their exchange. Rory found MacVurich lying drunk in a local hostelry and announced:

Tha Domhnall odhar an diu gu tinn	Sallow Donald is sick today
cur fos a chinn an taigh an oil	Throwing up in the tavern
ge be dhiolas an lach air a shon	Whoever pays the lawing for him,
ni e biadh do choin Mhic Leoid.	He provides a meal for MacLeod's dogs.

Though obviously much the worse for drink, Donald's wits do not seem to have been too much blunted, and he replied :

Chuir thus' athais air Mac Leoid	You have given affront to MacLeod
nach coir dhomh-sa bhith dha chleith,	that I ought not to conceal,
mur faigh a chuid con de lon	If his dogs can find no food
ach na ni luchd oil do sgeith	save what drunkards vomit.
Is olc am fasan do Mac Leoid,	It is bad policy for MacLeod
ged as toigh leis fearas-theud,	though he is found of harp music.
luchd foille bhith aige m'a bhord,	to have a treacherous crew round his table,
doilleirean gun phaidir gun chreud.	darkened minds without Pater Noster or Creed.
Comhairle uam-sa do 'n tighearn	My advice to the Laird
Sliochd a' Bhritheimh a dhearmad,	is to shun the Lawman's offspring.
siol nam murt is na h-eiceirt	a race given to murder and injustice
a bha droch eucail a' leanmhainn	ever marked by an evil disposition.
Cha bu chuilean de 'n t-seorsa	A whelp of that breed
as am bu choir a bhith 'g earbsa,	ought not to be trusted
gun fios nach cinneadh fo mheuraibh	as there's no knowing but there might
"Deuchainn-ghleusda Mhic O Charmaig".	sound forth under his fingers
	"The Tuning-trial of Mac O Charmaig".

This speech is full of references to past untrustworthiness of the Harper's own clan and the treachery of harpers, one of whom, according to legend, had attempted to murder a MacLeod chief! (See Note 2).

Not all such poetic contests ended in animosity, however. There is a story in a "History of Kintyre" by Peter Macintosh (1861) about William McMurchy (c1700-78) who was a harper as well as a piper and poet. "William McMurchy who lived at Largieside about a century ago was a superior piper and poet. He was visited by a learned gentleman who came in disguise to test McMurchy's power of poetry, the gentleman himself being a poet. McMurchy received the gentleman in a respectful manner and entertained him with a few tunes on his pipes. The gentleman was musing over a verse of poetry, and observing some scones of bread toasting over the fire, got up hurriedly and making for the door uttered :

Piobaireachd is aran tur,	Piping and raw bread,
'S miosa leam na guin a bhais,	worse to me than pangs of death.
Fhir a bhodhair mo dha chluais,	Ye man who deaved both my ears,
Na biodh agad duais gu brach.	may you never get a reward.

McMurchy dropping the pipe out of his mouth rapidly said :

Stad a dhuine fan ri cial,	Stop man give ear to reason,
'S olc an sgial nach boin ri bun,	bad is the story that has no foundation.
Tha mo bhean a t-eachd on Chill,	My wife is coming from Chil
Is ultach d'on im air a muin.	with a load of butter on her back.

The gentleman finding that he had met his match returned and a friendly conversation took place till McMurchy's wife came home with the butter. The gentleman partook of the toasted bread and butter and came away wondering that such a man as McMurchy could be found in such a sequestered spot".

Keith Sanger has pointed out other reference to rivalry, not to say violence, between harpers and fiddlers. The Burgh records of Edinburgh (27th September, 1594) mention that Baillie Clement Kerr had handed over to the Treasurer a purse containing six pounds and ten shillings. The purse had belonged to Ogilby, a fiddler, who had been executed for the murder of a harper named Caldell.

Another violent exchange is detailed in the papers of the Laird of Grant who wrote in 1638 to his agent in Ayr enquiring why his "Clairschear" had failed to return from a visit to the Lowlands. The agent, John Donaldson, explained that there had been a drunken fight between the "Clairschear" and a Violer named John Hay which had left the violer "very ill hurt in the head, where out of there is two bones come, and it is in doubt if ever he will be well". The clarsach player was "hurt in the hand; where he is or how he will be I can not learn, for I have not been very curious to ask". Perhaps the relative extent of their injuries would be consistent with supposing that the two musicians had struck each other with their respective instruments!

86

18. **Cumha Peathar Ruaidhri** (Lament for Rory's Sister)

Daniel Dow published this tune in his "Collection of Ancient Scots Music". As with "Fuath nam Fidhleirean", William Matheson argues that since this tune is ascribed in Dow's book to Rory Dall, while "Port Lennox", "Port Gordon" and "Port Atholl" appear in the same collection without ascription, they seem, in Dow's view, to have different origins. The three "Ports" are included in Bowie's Collection and in that the composer is named as "Rory Daul", while Bowie does not include "Cumha Peathar Ruaidhri", "Fuath nam Fidhleirean", "Is eagal leam am Bas" or "Suipear Tighearna Leoid". Arthur O'Neill, the Irish harper (1734-1818) does not name these four tunes in his list of Ruaidhri Dall O'Cathain's compositions. It does seem possible that this tune, therefore, may be one composed by Rory Morison.

On the other hand, however, the Blind Harper is known to have had only one sister, who survived him. It has been suggested that he might have had a sister who died in infancy who was not mentioned in any of the family records or traditions. There is also a mention of a sister belonging to the Irish Ruairi O'Cahan who is described in "Dalriada : or North Antrim" by William Adams. His father, Gilladuff or An Giolla Dubh O'Cahan is said to have had three, possibly four, sons mentioned in various sources, and a daughter who married a Henry MacHenry. Of course, the female side of the family was of much less importance to historians at this period so their lives are difficult to trace.

I have a further suggestion to make which would accord with the tune being the composition of Rory Morison. The title of the tune in Gaelic is "Cumha Peathar Ruaidhri", "The Lament for Rory's Sister". Only in the English translation is it given as Rory <u>Dall's</u> sister. The young chief who succeeded his father in 1693 was also called Ruaidhri. He did have sisters, one of whom, Iseabail, married Robert Stewart of Appin. She apparently died before 1710 when Robert Stewart remarried. It might well be that the Blind Harper would compose a lament for his chief's sister, even though Ruaidhri Og MacLeod himself died in 1699. She would almost certainly have known the Harper well as a member of her father's household and may even have been on intimate terms with him as a friend, as Silis na Ceapaich was with Lachlann Dall. In addition, Rory Dall himself moved to Lochaber in 1700, relatively close to Appin, and may have had contact with her at this time, near the end of her life.

19. **Far-fuadach a' Chlarsair** (The Harper's Dismissal)

This little tune comes from the Angus Fraser manuscript and is a variant of the melody of the Blind Harper's song "Oran do Mhac Leiod Dhun Bheagain". This song was addressed to the young chief, Rory, shortly after his father's death. It describes the life at Dunvegan in the time of Iain Breac, and how times have now changed,

Tha Mac-alla fo ghruaim
anns an talla 'm biodh fuaim a' cheoil
'n ionad tathaich nan cliar,
gun aighear, gun mhiadh, gun phoit,
gun mhire, gun mhuirn,
gun iomartas dluth nan corn,
gun chuirm, gun phailteas ri daimh,
gun mhacnas, gun mhanran beoil.

Echo is dejected in the hall where music was wont to sound, in the place resorted to by poet-bands, now without mirth, or pleasure, or drinking, without merriment or entertainment, without the passing round of drinking-horns in close succession, without feasting, without liberality to men of learning, without dalliance, or voice raised in tuneful song.

and how he took part himself

An trath chuirte 'na tamh i
le furtachd 'na fardaich fein,
dhomh-sa b'fhurasd' a radh
gum bu chuireideach gair nan teud,
le h-iomairt dha-lamh
cur am binnis do chach an ceill:
righ, bu shiubhlach ri m' chluais
an luthadh le luasgan mheur.

When it (the bagpipe) was relieved and laid to rest in its own quarters, I could readily relate how beguiling was the sound of harp-strings, impressing all with their sweetness, under the play of two hands. Ah me! how fluent was the quick measure played close to my ear by swiftly moving fingers.

Now, he says, the young chief is squandering the family's money on fine living and gambling, in the Lowlands, and Dunvegan is without music.

It has been widely assumed that it was because of dislike for Rory Og that the Blind Harper left Dunvegan. This may have been part of the reason, but William Matheson points out that he had removed far from Skye, to Glenelg, in the lifetime of Iain Breac. Matheson suggests that this was because of the harper's well-known allegiance to the Jacobite cause, which he was apt to voice publicly, and that this may have been an embarrassment to his patron, trying to retain a neutral stance, while pressure was brought to bear on him to call out the clan to join Viscount Dundee's army in support of James II.

Rory Dall was sent to part of the MacLeod lands called Totamor, in Glenelg, where he owned a herd of cattle, and was apparently given the land rent-free, Matheson suggests, in order to soften the blow of his banishment. During this period Rory found another patron in John MacLeod of Talisker, who he also esteemed highly as a friend, as we see in his "Lament for the Goodman of Talisker". Talisker apparently attracted a number of poets and musicians, like Iain macAilein (John Maclean), a poet, and the Blind Piper, John Mackay, who had studied with Patrick Og MacCrimmon in Skye. The Harper's banishment, then, was not without its comfort of friendship and shared culture.

20. **The Lament for the Harp Key** (Cumha Crann nan Teud)

This tune has a fascinating and tangled background. It is played today as a great piece of ceol mor on the pipes under the title "Cumha Craobh nan Teud" or "The Lament for the Harp Tree". This title does not make sense. It does seem likely that the Gaelic word "craobh" meaning "tree" has been substituted at some point for the word "crann" which has the double meaning of "tree" and "harp-key". The title "Lament for the Harp Key" still seems rather obscure. There is a traditional story that the Blind Harper, Rory Morison, lost his harp-key amongst the ashes of the fire one day in MacLeod's household but this does not seem to me to justify the feeling behind this great melody. This tune is often attributed to Rory Morison and he certainly wrote a song for which the words still exist called "Feill nan Crann" "The Harp-Key Fair" about the loss of his harp-key and the efforts of the women of the household to find it, which involved a voyage to Barra. In this poem the harp-key is clearly used as a phallic symbol. This seems to have been a common poetic metaphor which would perhaps suggest itself as a subject for piobaireachd. William Matheson has also pointed out that with a slight change in melodic stress the words of "Feill nam Crann" fit the first part of the ground of the pipe tune. On the other hand, the pipers and harpers had mutual respect at this time and the tune may simply be seen as a lament for the loss of a great musical tradition at a time when the harp was dying out in Scotland.

Angus Fraser gives a version of the tune which he says is closer to the vocal setting of the melody, than the pipe setting published by Angus Mackay. Fraser says that it was sung under the title "A Bhean Sith" or "An Leannan Sith" ("The Fairy Woman/Lover). There is also another pipe tune called "Failte Choire an Easa", "Corrienessan's Salute", a fragrant of a piobaireachd,tigh which is clearly another version of the same tune. Interestingly, in a poem "Cumha Coire an Easa" by John Mackay, the Blind Piper, he describes a hunting party at Coire an Easa (The Corry of the Waterfall) in Reay country in Caithness. This took place sometime between 1689 and 1696. Mackay says, speaking as the corry itself :

> Bu lionmhor de mhaithean na h-Eireann
> thigeadh gu m' reidhlean le h-ealaidh;
> sheinneadh Ruaidhri Dall dhomh failte,
> bhiodh MacAoidh 's a chairdean mar ris
>
> Many of the nobles of Ireland
> would come to my green sward in merry mood;
> Blind Rory would play a salute to me
> Mackay and his friends would be with him.

The title of the tune that Rory Dall played here would have been "Failte Choire an Easa" ("Corrienessan's Salute"?). It seems obvious that this tune was known and played by both pipers and harpers. There was no rivalry between these two instruments (as there apparently was between the harpers and fiddle players) and pipers and harpers alike obviously knew a good tune when they heard it!

The relationship between harp music and the ceol mor of the pipes is interesting. There seems little doubt that the harp had a form of music based on a theme with variations, similar to piobaireachd. Many of the known harp tunes in the old collections include variations, and those tunes composed by later musicians, supposedly in an old harp style, often have variations which the composers obviously see as characteristic of this kind of music. It is noticeable that the only two tunes of O Carolan's which have variations are based on Scottish themes.

Adding variations to a melody is not, of course, a purely traditional idea, and many examples are found in classical music and in classically influenced traditional music, such as 17th century Scottish lute music, some of the 18th century Scottish fiddle music and some Irish harp music of the late 18th century and early 19th century. These variations, however, are usually fairly obvious in their classical construction. The characteristically Scottish variation in traditional music depends, it seems to me, on simplifying the notes of a slow air, to a basic structure, which can then be altered rhythmically and made more complicated by decorating these basic notes. These notes are also often doubled or repeated but always remain prominent.

There is a great deal of research and discussion going on at present about the origins of piobaireachd, but it seems likely that it did not become formalised into the present structure until around the beginning of the 19th century. It may have been played in a rather freer form previous to that, but there seems to be no doubt that this great music was accepted for hundreds of years as being an appropriate form of expression of high emotion or to mark significant events.

Another interesting link is found in the analysis of piobaireachd structure suggested by Alex Haddow and John Macfadyen. Taking the tune as a 2-bar phrase, they brought it down to a formula of A A B A
B B A B
In the early 17th century Welsh manuscript by ap Huw, which lists the 24 measures of Welsh harp music (described in terms of 1 and 0), he gives one called "Alban Hyfaidd" ("Scottish Tuning"). If this is written out next to Haddow and Macfadyen's formula, it can be seen to be an exact mirror image. Thus:

"Alban Hyfaidd"   1 0 1 1   A A B A
                         0 1 0 0   B B A B
                         0 1 0 0   B B A B)
                         1 0 1 1   A A B A) inversion of first group

This parallel was pointed out to me by Keith Sanger and may be pure coincidence, but even so, it is a fascinating one.

I have chosen to arrange the Angus Fraser melody, and have added three of my own variations. These are closer to the pipe treatment of the tune rather than basing them on Fraser's which, he states, were "revised for pianoforte" by himself.

This is not the arrangement, made by Francis Collinson, which I recorded on my first album "The Harp Key".

The decorations should be played exactly as I have written them as they form an integral part of the ringing harmony.

21. Ellen's Dreams

The following two tunes are my own family's contribution to the clarsach's repertoire. "Ellen's Dreams" was written by my husband, Robin Morton, for our daughter, Ellen, and is a most beautiful melody. It has a rather Irish feel about it, which is not surprising since Robin comes from Portadown in Co. Armagh, Northern Ireland. Incidentally, this was also the birthplace of Patrick Quin, a harper who took part in the famous harp festival in Belfast in 1792. I had already used the title "Ellen's Dreams" for a piece of crystal which I had engraved for Ellen when she was a baby.

The illustration shows a block of crystal, designed and engraved by Alison Kinnaird, entitled "Ellen's Dreams".

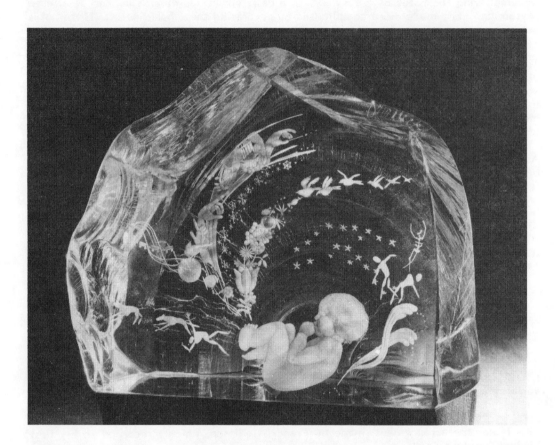

22. The Braidwood Waits

I composed "The Braidwood Waits" as a present for Robin whose birthday falls on Christmas Eve. "Braidwood" is the small group of houses where we live, just outside the village of Temple in Midlothian. The "Waits" were travelling musicians. Chambers says in his "Book of Days" - "A remnant of this custom, still popularly called "waits", yet exists in the magistrates of the City of Glasgow annually granting a kind of certificate or diploma to a few musicians, generally blind men of respectable character, who perambulate the streets of the city during the night or morning for about three weeks or a month previous to New Year's Day, in most cases performing on violins the slow, soothing airs peculiar to a portion of the old Scottish melodies; and in the solemn silence of repose the effect is very fine".

23. Sheuglie's Contest betwixt his Harp, Fiddle and Pipes

Alexander Grant of Shewglie was born around 1675, and became well-known during the 1745 Jacobite Rising when he was seized and imprisoned in Inverness by Grant of Grant. Shewglie had not taken part in the Rising – he was about 70 years old – and had apparently persuaded some of the rebels in Urquhart to lay down their arms. However, his connections were strongly Jacobite and he had composed a number of poems, among which was a welcome to Prince Charles in 1745 "Do bheatha Thearlaich Stiubhart, Do bheatha ar duthaich". He was also accused of carrying messages for the Young Pretender. In prison Shewglie became seriously ill and was released to a more comfortable confinement but died of a fever in July, 1746.

Shewglie is said to have played Harp, Pipes and Fiddle and composed a poem "Mairi Nighean Deorsa" addressed to his fiddle which appears in Daniel Dow's and Simon Fraser's collections. In the latter it is called "Sheuglie's Contest betwixt his Harp, Fiddle and Pipes" and the notes describe it as having been acquired by the editor's grandfather from a successor of the composer. The notes give some brief translation of the verses in which Shewglie imagines the three instruments have quarrelled. He is called on to decide the contest and describes the qualities of each instrument. "In addressing a verse to his pipe, he observes 'how it would delight him, on hearing the sound of war, to listen to her notes, in striking up the gathering, to rally round the chief, on a frosty spring morning, whilst the hard earth reverberated all her notes, so as to be heard by the most distant person interested'. To the harp he says – 'The pleasure which thy tones afford are doubled, whilst accompanying a sweet female voice, or round the festive board, inspired by love or wine, I reach beyond my ordinary capacity, and feel the pleasure of pleasing.' But to his violin, which he calls by the literal name of the air "Mary, George's Daughter", and seems to have been his favourite, though held cheap by other combatants, he says – 'I love thee, for the sake of those who do – the sprightly youth and bonny lasses – all of whom declare, that, at a wedding, dance or ball, thou with thy bass in attendance, can have no competitor – thy music having the effect of electricity on those who listen to it' – and on thus receiving their due share of praise, their reconciliation is convivially celebrated" (Simon Fraser).

Two other Gaelic poets used this name for the fiddle, and the same air. Alasdair Og MacDonald, Fir Ardnabighe, wrote a song to the fiddle which begins "Gum b'ait Leam 'bhi lamh-ruit A Mhairi nigh 'n Deorsa" and in reply Alexander MacDonald composed a poem in praise of his pipes. The idea of a "flyting " – a poetic boasting quarrel – seems to have been a popular one even at this date. Unfortunately, Shewglie's poem in the original Gaelic has been lost and we are now only left with the partial English translation in Fraser's notes. If a version of Shewglie's poem could be found, it could throw considerable light on the attitudes towards the harp in the early part of the 18th century during a period in which the instrument was undergoing rapid decline.

24. The Keiking Glasse

The harp was an instrument widely used at the Court of the Kings and Queens of Scotland. Indeed, several of them, including James I, James IV and Mary, Queen of Scots, are said to have played it themselves. James I is said to have touched it "like another Orpheus" and that "on the harp he excelled the Irish or the Highland Scots, who are esteemed the best performers on that instrument". A great deal of flattery obviously went on at Court!

In the Royal Accounts of James III, which survive from 1473, we have numerous mentions of payments to harpers at Court, and heard performing for the King throughout Scotland from Dingwall and Elgin in the North to Wigtown and Linlithgow in the Lowlands. James V also, in the small section of his accounts which have been published, made many payments to musicians. Francis Collinson suggests that the names harp and clarsach were used interchangeably and did not represent the gut-strung and wire-strung instruments respectively. But there are entries such as :
"1501 April 13th, Pate harpar on the harp, Pate harper on the clarsach, James Mylson harpar, the Ireland clarscha, and an English harpar, each received xiiijs".

There appear to have been two "Pates", the elder playing the "clarsach" and his son who played the "harp". Whether the two names are used to differentiate between father and son or that they both played different instruments is not clear. Most of the entries for Highland and Irish musicians (who traditionally are said to have played only wire-strung instruments) are indeed for "Ersch (i.e. Erse or Gaelic) clarsacha" "Irish clarscha" or "Ersch clarscharis" but there are also references to "ane Ersche harpar" and "Odonelis (O'Donnell's) harpar quhilk past away with him". So we cannot draw any firm conclusions about which instrument was being played. We do know that both gut-strung and wire-strung harps have probably been played in Scotland since at least the early 16th century.

This tune comes from the Skene Manuscript, an early 17th century manuscript which is written in lute tablature, which contains some other harp tunes. This one attracted me because it fits well on the harp and I liked the way it expressed the "Mirror" image of the title, which is Scots for "Looking Glass". Some years later, Bonnie Shaljean noticed that the same tune occurs, in a different version, as the unnamed "Port 1st" in the harp-tunes of the Maclean-Clephane Manuscript so it is rather nice to have one's instinct of possible harp tunes confirmed!

I arranged it as a quartet for clarsach, harpsichord, fiddle and viola, which makes a lovely combination of sounds and rather suits the period of the melody. The parts are very simple, but the ensemble texture is surprisingly rich.

The illustration shows a detail of the painted ceiling at Crathes Castle.
By kind permission of the National Trust for Scotland.
Photo by Country Life Magazine.

SOURCES FOR TUNES

Bowie, John –

A Collection of Strathspey Reels & Country Dances c. 1780 (National Library of Scotland).

Bunting, Edward –

The Ancient Music of Ireland – Dublin 1840 (reprinted Walton's Piano & Musical Instrument Galleries, Dublin. 1969)

Dauney, William –

Ancient Scotish Melodies 1838 (transcription of Skene Manuscript, National Library of Scotland)

Dow, Daniel –

A Collection of Ancient Scots Music c.1778 (National Library of Scotland)

Fraser, Angus –

M.S. Collection (Edinburgh University Library)

Fraser, Capt. Simon –

The Airs and Melodies Peculiar to the Highlands of Scotland and the Isles (reprinted Paul Cranford, Sydney, Nova Scotia, 1982)

McDonald, Patrick –

A Collection of Highland Vocal Airs 1784 (reprinted Norwood Editions, Norwood, P.A., U.S.A. 1973)

MacFarlan, Walter –

M.S. c.1742 (National Library of Scotland)

Maclean-Clephane –

M.S. (National Library of Scotland)

Matheson, William –

The Blind Harper (Scottish Gaelic Texts Society, Edinburgh 1970)

Noble, Lt. Alexander –

M.S. 1813 (Unpublished. Copy in author's collection)

Oswald, James –

A Caledonian Pocket Companion 1745–59 (National Library of Scotland)

Straloch M.S. –

National Library of Scotland.

OTHER PUBLICATIONS OF BACKGROUND INTEREST

Armstrong, Robert –   The Irish & Highland Harps (Edinburgh 1904)
                                       (Reprinted Irish University Press 1969)

Black, Ronald –   "Colla Ciotach". Transactions of the Gaelic Society
                                       of Inverness Vol. 48 1972–74

Boswell's Journal of a Tour to the Hebrides

Campbell, Alexander –   A slight sketch of a journey made through parts
                                       of the Highlands and Hebrides 1815 (Manuscript
                                       Edinburgh University Library)

Collinson, Francis –   The Traditional & National Music of Scotland (R.K.P.
                                       1966)

Ferguson, Macdonald, Gillespie
London –   From the Farthest Hebrides 1978

Gunn, John –   An Historical Enquiry respecting the Performance
                                       of the Harp 1807.

MacKenzie, Annie ed. –   Oran Iain Luim (Scottish Gaelic Texts Society
                                       Edinburgh 1964)

Matheson, William –   The Blind Harper (Scottish Gaelic Texts Society
                                       Edinburgh 1970)

Moncrieffe & Hicks –   The Highland Clans 1967

O'Baoill, Dr. Colm –   Some Irish Harpers (transactions of the Gaelic
                                       Society of Inverness Vol. 47)

O'Sullivan –   Carolan – The Life & Times of an Irish Harper
                                       – London

Sanger, Keith –   Some Unruly Scottish Harpers (Folk Harp Journal
                                       No. 47 – Dec. 1984)

Sanger, Keith –   Argylls Retainers (Society for West Highland &
                                       Island Historical Research No. 22, 1983)

Sanger, Keith –   William McMurchy – Piping Times Vol. 34, No.1
                                       1981.

Yeats, Grainne –   Some thoughts on Irish Harp Music 'Ceol' IV (2)
                                       1973

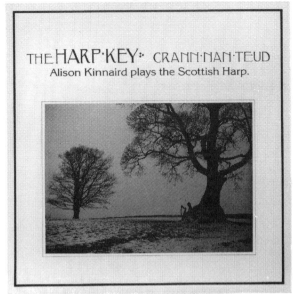
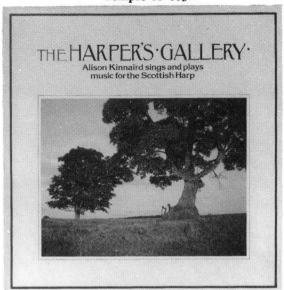

Drawing of Alison Kinnaird's hands and jacket design by John Haxby–Edinburgh